Found one!

even

Great work!

Purple Ronnie's

♡ Guide for ♡

LOVERS

♡

by Purple Ronnie

Purple Ronnie's Little Book of Pants first published 1999 by Boxtree
Purple Ronnie's Little Book of Willies and Bottoms first published 1999 by Boxtree
Purple Ronnie's Little Guide for Lovers first published 1999 by Boxtree
Purple Ronnie's Little Guide to Doing It first published 1999 by Boxtree
This omnibus edition published 2003 for Index by Boxtree
an imprint of PanMacmillan Publishers Ltd.
20 New Wharf Road
London N1 9RR

www.macmillan.com

Associated companies throughout the world

ISBN 0 7522 2507 3

A CIP catalogue record for this book is
available from the British Library

Text by Giles Andreae
Illustrations by Janet Cronin
Printed and Bound by Bath Press

Men's Pants

ooh

a poem about
↓
Men's Pants

Some men wear pants that are sexy
and tight

And some men wear pants that are
stringy

But some men go round with no pants
on at all

Cos they're just so in love with
their Thingy

Posh Pants

← smart
silky
stuff

long
legs →

← baggy
bottoms

What men think: "I like having it swinging around"

What girls think: "I can't tell how big your thingy is"

Be careful when you are wearing Posh Pants because your willy can come peering out of them without you noticing

Willy Huggers

gleam

stretchy shiny stuff →

← super-snug fit

What men think: "I look like a sports god!"

What girls think: "Why is your thingy so knobbly?"

Warning: If you wear Willy Huggers for too long your voice goes all high and squeaky

whoah!

strain

jiggle

Grandad Pants

v. baggy

see-through stringy stuff

← moth-eaten holes

What men think: "They'll be back in fashion one day my boy!"

What girls think: "Aah, how sweet!"

Men who wear grandad pants haven't even got the tiniest chance of pulling, but they're probably more interested in gardening anyway

"when I was your age... blah... blah..."

Trendy Pants

designer name on waistband ←

KEVIN CLINE · KEVIN C

botty →
hugging
shape

What men think: "Do I look like those blokes in the ads?"

What girls think: "Why don't you look like those blokes in the ads?"

Trendy pants are good at keeping your bits in place, but they do make them rather sweaty

oo...er

itch

scratch

steam

Girly Pants

manly slogan

girly shape

teeny sack

What men think : "These feel a bit slinky!"

What girls think: "Why are you wearing my pants?"

Because loads of men like wearing girls' pants, pant shops pretend that some girls' pants are men's pants, but they're not - they're girls' pants

fab!

MANLY MEN'S PANTS IN MANLY MEN'S COLOURS

girls' pants

Y-Front Pants

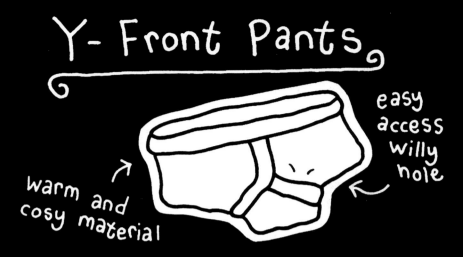

warm and cosy material

easy access willy hole

What men think: "Am I turning into my dad?"

What girls think: "I've got a headache!"

all-time king of pants

Y-Front Pant wearers are always great lovers because they don't need sexy pants to make girls want them

Posing Pants

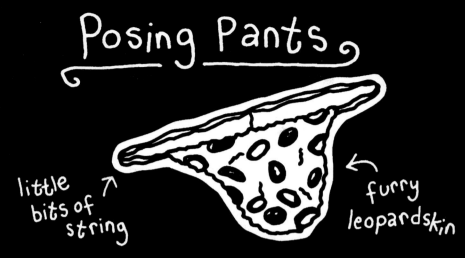

little bits of string

furry leopardskin

What men think: "Doesn't my packet look fab!"

What girls think: "Aagh! Scary!"

Posing Pants are worn by men with tiny willies who don't think they can pull without wrapping their bits up like a parcel

get 'em off!

strip

wiggle

Cod Pants

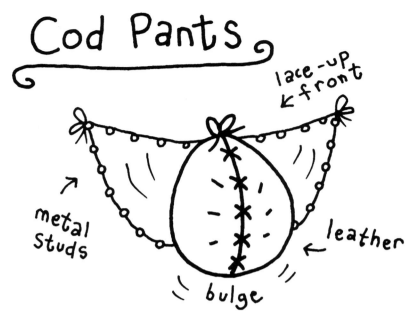

lace-up front

metal studs

leather

bulge

What men think: "I wish I was born 400 years ago!"

What girls think: "You should be in prison"

Cod Pants were worn by men in medieval times. Once you had strapped them on you could stuff loads of vegetables down the front to make your packet look enormous

hi girls!

squash

Space Pants

What men think: "At last, the ultimate gadget!"

What girls think "Men are weird!"

In the future, Space Pants will be able to do anything you want them to

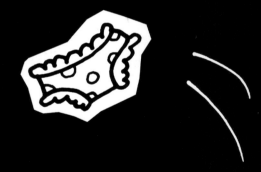

Girls' Pants

rummage

a poem about
Girls' Pants

Some girls wear huge comfy pants
That help them to relax
But others wear small stringy
                    ones
That go right up their cracks

girls in
their pants

tug

comfy

ooh!

squeeze

stringy

Granny Pants

loads of frilly bits

huge billowy legs →

What girls think: "I look like the star of an old soppy movie!"

What men think: "Aaagh! You look like my gran!"

People who wear Granny Pants are usually very shy about showing their bottoms

no peeping!

squidgey bum

hop hop

Up-Yer-Bum Pants

titchy
piece
of material ↗

tiny
stringy
bit ←

what girls think: "No one can see if I'm wearing any pants!"

what men think: "Hey! No pants!"

Up-Yer-Bum Pants are usually only worn by skinny people. Lardy bottoms do not look good in Up-Yer-Bums

wobble-free
bottom
↓

Pulling Pants

What girls think: "I know they're tarty but they work every time!"

What men think: "Get 'em off!"

Pulling Pants were invented to make men's trousers explode

Squashing Pants

super-strong material →

anti-flab ← bits

What girls think: "Ooh look, I'm 2 sizes smaller!"

What men think: "What are those bulgy bits at the top of your pants?"

Squashing Pants were invented to make your tummy look smaller. Do not wear them for too long or you might stop breathing

gasp!

faint

strain

squeeze

Work Pants

hole

used to be
stretchy

greyish
colour

no
frilly
bits

What girls think: "No one will see
them so it doesn't matter"

What men think: "Yuck!"

rush

I'm
late!

TEA

Work Pants are what you wear when you
can't be bothered to find anything else

Slinky Pants

slippery silky stuff →

What girls think: "Ooh... these are nice and breezy!"

What men think: "Classy bird!"

The only point of wearing slinky pants is for other people to see them

Slinky Pants are usually only given as presents by boyfriends

Spray-On Pants

tight and stretchy thin stuff ↗

skin coloured ↖

What girls think: "what a great invention!"

What men think: "What are <u>they</u> for?"

Spray-On Pants are best under really tight dresses. Never let a boy try on your Spray-Ons or they will burst

Love Pants

pretty flowers

soppy love hearts

What girls think: "I feel all pretty and girly!"

What men think: "I wonder if she'll ever let me Do It with her?"

Love Pants are worn by people who like to cuddle a lot

Mummy Pants

loads of room ↓

← ancient

v. comfy ↗

What girls think: "Do I know him well enough to wear these?"

what men think: "I wonder what's on telly?"

Mummy Pants should only be worn if you have been Doing It with the same person for at least 10 years

Warning:-

Willies hardly ever
behave the way you
want them to

...uh...oh

When you want your willy to be asleep...

when you want your willy to be awake...

...it falls asleep

Men's Bits

Men's Bits come in all sorts of shapes and sizes...

carrot

marrow

peanut

turnip

... and there are millions of different words for them

Todger
Winkle
Doodah
Dangler
Goolies
Wobbler
Plonker
Zobber

a poem about
Droopy Bits

Drinking makes men get all frisky
And chuck off their clothes in
a heap

They then want to Do It like crazy
But find that their Thingie's
asleep

a poem about
Men's Bits

Men's Bits sometimes look like bananas
And sometimes like shrivelled up grapes
But however they try
They just can't deny
That they come in the silliest shapes

Tip for Girls

Men with big cars hardly ever have big willies

a poem about a
Trouser Snake

Men give names like
Trouser Snake
To bits they use in bed
But snakes are very big
I'd call them
Trouser **Worms** instead

Tip for Men

Remember always to keep your privates nice and clean

a poem about
Bottoms

Some people's bottoms are skinny
and small

And some are all fat and enormous

Some are all hairy and covered in
spots

But yours is just totally

gorgeous

titter

smashing
botty

worship

☆ Special Tip
about Girls' Bottoms ☆

Always tell girls their
bottoms are amazing

If you hesitate for a
second - You've had it

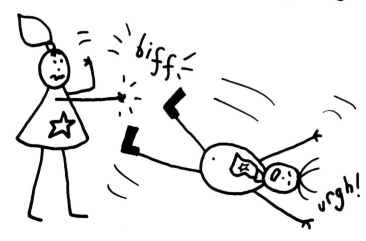

a poem about a
Squidgey Bum

Some people will do anything
To have a skinny bum
But what I like
Is a smiley face
And a nice fat squidgey <u>Bum</u>

lovely
smile

Squeeze

☆ Secret Note ☆

Front Bottoms

Only girls have Front Bottoms

← A Girl

Front Bottoms are too rude to talk about...

...I just wanted to say it

The most amazing
thing you can do with
your bottom is
Bottom Burping

a poem about
Bottom Burps

If your BOTTOM burps in public
Try to say in time
"Goodness gracious
what a whiff
It doesn't smell like mine"

a poem about being
Silent but Deadly

They're silent as a tiny mouse
They do not make a sound
They warm up in your
                    trouser leg
Then waft for miles around

tum te tum

← v.crafty

pong

sneaking out

First Rule of Bottom Burps

Your own Bottom Burps smell fantastic

mmmm

Other people's Bottom Burps smell disgusting

{gasp}

choke

poison

stagger

another poem about
Bottom↓Burps

Some people screw up their faces
And let out their farts bit by bit
Some people hope that they'll
creep back inside
But it's great fun to let them
just rip

a poem about
The Lav

Of all the most fabulous things
                        I can do
And the smashingest times I can
                        have
There isn't a pleasure I love quite
                        as much
As settling down on the Lav

Lovers

♡

a poem about
Safe Sex

To make sure you're safe when
you DO IT

Put on a Thingie that fits
I like the ones that can glow
in the dark
With the slippery nobbly bits

Girls Beware:-

Most men need a lesson in how to make you feel special

Being Fancied

If you want people to fancy you - it is best to be as mysterious as possible

a poem about
↓
Sex

Some people are just hopeless
When you get them in the sack
They'd always rather watch T.V.
Or have a boring chat

Men Beware :-

Girls always have sneaky ways of catching the men they fancy

Important :-

Try not to dribble too much when you are snogging...

...dribbling is not sexy

a poem about

Loving You

How many ways do I love you?
I think there are probably two
The rumpety-pump way
Is all very well
But I like the soppy way too

s.l.o.w

m.o.t.i.o.n

soft

focus

a poem about
Snogging

It's funny how us people
Show our love by touching tongues
But at least we're not all doggies
Or we'd sniff each others' <u>bums</u>!

Remember :-

Everyone has secret places where they like to be touched...

... find out where your Lover's are

Special Tip for Men

Girls like their lovers to be romantic and exciting...

...It is not <u>always</u> best to be incredibly skilful

a poem about
Love Handles

Some people think they're not
sexy
Unless they're as skinny as
candles
But I think it feels much nicer
To cuddle some squidgey
Love Handles

Positions

You can Do It in all sorts of different positions

... some are more complicated than others

a poem to say
I Love You

Sometimes when it's late at night
And we're alone together
I want to take you in my arms
And cuddle you forever

...give your lover
treats and surprises

a poem for
My Scrumptious Lover

You're so unbelievably gorgeous
I thought that I'd just have to say
I'd love to submerge you in chocolate
And lick it off slowly all day

a poem about
Kiss̆ing

Some kisses last for just seconds
They're gentle and go on the
                           cheeks
But I like the ones you put right
                       on the lips
That can go on for 2 or 3 weeks

Naughty Tip

Spice up your love life with new tricks...

... but try not to go too far

Special Tip for Men

Try not to fart and fall asleep straight after Doing It...

...most girls do not like that

Special Tip for Girls

If you tell a man he is brilliant in bed...

...he will do anything for you

a not too soppy poem to say

I Love You

This poem says I love you
And you make my life complete
Except for all your bottom burps
And your stinky feet

a poem for a
Lover

If someone invented a gadget

That made me terrific in bed

I think I'd buy twenty-five
                         thousand

And Do It with you till I'm dead

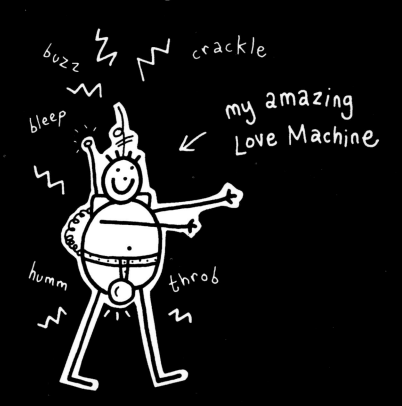

buzz

crackle

bleep

my amazing
Love Machine

humm

throb

DOING IT ♡

Things You Will Need

There are only 2 things you need for Doing It

Boys

Girls

a willy →

← a front bottom

They are both quite hard to leave behind

a poem about

Foreplay

Some men like to nibble
And some men like to stroke

But others simply drop their pants
And shout "let's have a poke!"

Getting in the Mood

Music is a great way of getting people in the mood for Doing It...

... make sure you get the right sort

Being Bare

Most people like to be bare when they are Doing It

It is best not to laugh when they take their clothes off

a poem about
Willies

When girls say that size doesn't
matter
You know they don't mean it
at all
It's just a polite way of saying
That yours is incredibly small

Be Nice

Good lovers always make sure that the other person is having a nice time too

Special Tip

Doing It on the floor can be fun, but try not to get carpet burns on your bottom

a poem about
Girls

Some girls hide under the duvet
Then peel off their clothes bit
by bit
But others love flaunting their
gorgeous basoomers
And instantly dropping their
kit

Shouting Names

Some people get turned on if you shout out their name while you're Doing It...

... make sure you know what they are called first.

Special Tip

There are lots of things you can find in the kitchen that make Doing It even more exciting

Good Things

yum yum!

Bad Things

Yuk!

Outdoors

Doing It in public places can be fun but try to make sure they're not <u>too</u> public

a poem about ↓ Fantasies

Some girls dream they'll fall in
love
With aliens from Mars
But others just want rampant
sex
With oily men in cars

Safety

When Doing It with someone for the first time it is always best to use protection

Surprises

Some people make Doing It more exciting by taking their lover by surprise

The Shower

The best thing about Doing It in the shower...

...is that nobody has to sleep in the wet patch

a poem about
Doing It

Some people just love to Do It
In cars or in buses or trains
But nothing compares
To that feeling you get
When you shag in the lavvies
of planes

Things not to say while Doing It

Men

1. How's your Mum?

2. What's on telly?

3. Come on!

Girls

1. Is it in yet?

2. zzzzzz

3. Have you finished?

Special Trick

If you want to Do It with someone <u>really</u> sexy tell them it's their minds you fancy

Making It Last

Men sometimes need to think of something completely different to make it last

It is best not to tell girls what you are thinking of

After Doing It

You should always cuddle, hug and kiss for at least 10 minutes after Doing It...

...that way girls will know that you like them too.

a poem about

Loving

It's all very well to be hung like
a hippo

And make ladies squeal with delight

But sometimes they much prefer
someone who cares

To be holding them closely all night

in love